Career-Ready Kids

CREATE AND EXPERIENCE

Diane Lindsey Reeves

21st Century Junior Library

Published in the United States of America by:

Cherry Lake Press
2395 South Huron Parkway, Suite 200, Ann Arbor, Michigan 48104
www.cherrylakepress.com

Reading Adviser: Beth Walker Gambro, MS, Ed., Reading Consultant, Yorkville, IL

Photo Credits: © Pixel-Shot/Shutterstock, cover; Anastasia Shuraeva/Pexel.com, 5; cottonbro studio/Pexels.com, 6; © BlueOrange Studio/Shutterstock, 7; © Prostock-studio/Shutterstock, 8–9; © Seventyfourimages/Dreamstime.com, 10–11; © Media_Photos/Shutterstock, 13; © Hananeko_Studio/Shutterstock, 14; © SeventyFour/Shutterstock, 15; © Master1305/Shutterstock, 16; Nataliya Vaitkevich/Pexels.com, 19

Copyright © 2026 by Cherry Lake Publishing Group
All rights reserved. No part of this book may be reproduced or utilized in any form or by any means without written permission from the publisher.

Cherry Lake Press is an imprint of Cherry Lake Publishing Group.

Library of Congress Cataloging-in-Publication Data has been filed and is available at catalog.loc.gov.

Cherry Lake Publishing Group would like to acknowledge the work of the Partnership for 21st Century Learning, a Network of Battelle for Kids. Please visit Battelle for Kids online for more information.

Printed in the United States of America

Note from publisher: Websites change regularly, and their future contents are outside of our control. Supervise children when conducting any recommended online searches for extended learning opportunities.

CONTENTS

Chapter 1: Discover the Creating and Experiencing Career Cluster ... 4

Chapter 2: Explore Creating and Experiencing Careers ... 10

Chapter 3: Is Creating and Experiencing in Your Future? ... 17

Activity ... 21
Glossary ... 22
Find Out More ... 23
Index ... 24
About the Author ... 24

DISCOVER THE CREATING AND EXPERIENCING CAREER CLUSTER

Bring your imagination to the Creating and Experiencing cluster from the National Career Clusters® Framework. What's the number one skill for Creating careers? It's **creativity**, of course! Creativity also comes into play with Experiencing careers. This cluster has many **adventurous** options. But it's not all fun! These careers also require hard work.

The Creating and Experiencing cluster includes two groups. Some focus more on creativity. These include arts, entertainment, and design careers. Maybe you want to perform for an audience. Maybe you want to make music. Maybe you want to create art. These careers are all in this cluster.

Some careers in this cluster focus more on experiences. These are **hospitality**, events, and **tourism** careers.

You don't have to wait until you're an adult to try out some of these career ideas.

Look!

What kinds of entertainment careers have you seen in action lately? Did you know that you're seeing these careers in action every day? You see them whenever you watch a show, movie, or commercial. Look for them and you'll notice them everywhere.

Hospitality careers are at the hotels and resorts people stay in for business and pleasure. Events careers are part of business conferences. They're part of all kinds of festivals, concerts, and other special events. Careers in restaurants fit in this cluster, too.

Do you like to travel? Would you like to do it for your career one day?

Tourism careers offer interesting experiences for traveling. You could stick close to home or fly around the globe.

Let's explore the two Creating and Experiencing career areas:

- Arts, entertainment, and design
- Hospitality, events, and tourism

Create!

Thinking about a career in hospitality or events? Draw a picture of a kid-friendly hotel you would want to visit. Feature a fun event you could attend.

EXPLORE CREATING AND EXPERIENCING CAREERS

As you've read, the Creating and Experiencing career cluster has two groups of careers. The arts, entertainment, and design group is first. It has many careers for people to let their creative talent soar.

The arts include the ways people perform on stages and on screens. The arts also include all the careers that work behind the scenes. These careers include lighting experts. They include directors and makeup artists.

Behind-the-scenes careers keep everyone in the spotlight looking good.

Another side of the arts is fine arts. These include painting, sculpture, and more. Artists express creative skills and often make a living in many ways.

The literary arts are also a part of this group. Writers, authors, and journalists use words to entertain or inform. Publishers and editors bring this written work to the public.

Make a Guess!

Can you guess which Creating and Experiencing careers often show up on lists of dream careers for kids? Dancer, choreographer, actor, musician, and writer are favorites. All are fun choices. Just be sure to check out other careers in the Creating and Experiencing cluster.

When it comes to design, you can take your pick. Maybe you like fashion or interior design. Maybe you are into graphic design. Designers tell stories with pictures and style.

Wedding planner is a career that can make dreams come true! Is it right for you?

Hospitality, events, and tourism careers let the good times roll. They might provide comfortable places for travelers to stay. Or plan the wedding of a young couple's dreams. They could lead a busload of students on a tour of Washington, DC. Or organize a world tour for a rock band. There are so many ways to make a career out of making fun things happen.

Want a career in art that involves moving around a lot? Maybe dance will be for you!

IS CREATING AND EXPERIENCING IN YOUR FUTURE?

Are you creative and artsy? Always up for new experiences and adventure? If your answer is yes, that's a good clue! Creating and Experiencing careers might offer some good choices for you.

There is no rush to decide. But it can be fun to check out the options. Figure out what you like to do. Think of what you want to know more about.

These clues will help narrow down your choices. Learn about yourself and explore different careers. These are good ways to be a career-ready kid.

You can experiment with career ideas, too. Ask an adult to help you talk to someone with a career that interests you. An adult can help you visit places where these people work. Think about what the work is like. Imagine how you can add a little fun and beauty to the world.

Being a career-ready kid **motivates** you to do your best work now. You can build a bridge from learning in school to preparing for your future career.

Think!

Think about a major event like a Super Bowl game or Taylor Swift concert. What kinds of careers work behind the scenes to make them happen?

Talking to adults who have careers you admire is a great place to start. You might learn a thing or two!

INVESTIGATE CREATING AND EXPERIENCING CAREERS

Dramatic Arts and Music
- actor
- costume designer
- drama teacher
- sound engineer
- musician

Experiences
- activity director
- event planner
- tour guide

CREATE AND EXPERIENCE

Literary Arts
- editor
- journalist
- publisher
- writer

Visual Arts
- animator
- graphic designer
- sports photographer
- social media manager

Hospitality
- airline ticket agent
- cruise ship captain
- resort manager
- chef

ACTIVITY

Practice creating! Is there a problem you want to work through? Do you have some big feelings you want to think about? Creating can help you do these things. It can also bring more beauty into the world.

- Choose what art form you want to use to express yourself or problem-solve. Do you want to write a short story? Maybe you want to paint. Maybe you want to write a song. You could even choreograph a dance. The possibilities are endless.

- When you're done creating, you can decide if you want to share your art with others. You may want to keep it for yourself. It's up to you! The point is to have fun creating!

Ask Questions!

Who is your favorite entertainer in music or movies? What can you find out about how their career came to be? Are they doing what they dreamed of doing when they were a kid like you?

GLOSSARY

adventurous (uhd-VEN-chuh-ruhs) willing to try new, exciting, or difficult things

choreographer (kohr-ee-AH-gruh-fuhr) person who organizes steps and movements in a dance performance

creativity (kree-ay-TIH-vuh-tee) process of using imagination to think of new ideas

hospitality (hah-spuh-TAA-luh-tee) business of providing food, drinks, and lodging for guests

motivates (MOH-tuh-vayts) provides a person with a reason for taking action

tourism (TOOR-ih-zuhm) business of providing services for people who are traveling for pleasure

FIND OUT MORE

Books

Hodge, Susie. *I Like Art . . . What Jobs Are There?* Tulsa, OK: Kane Miller, 2021.

Martin, Steve. *I Like the Performing Arts . . . What Jobs Are There?* Tulsa, OK: Kane Miller, 2022.

Rauf, Don. *Choose Your Own Career Adventure: Hollywood.* Ann Arbor, MI: Cherry Lake, 2017.

Websites

Explore these online resources with an adult.

The Arty Teacher: Arts Careers

Time for Kids: Your Hot Job—Hospitality

INDEX

activities, 9, 21
arts careers, 6–7, 9–13, 16, 20

career choices, 6, 8, 12, 17–20
career clusters, 4, 6, 9–10
creating careers, 4–7, 9–13, 16–17, 20–21

design careers, 6, 9–10, 13, 20

entertainment careers, 6–7, 9–12, 16, 20–21
events careers, 6–7, 9, 14–15, 18, 20
experiencing careers, 4, 6–9, 14–15, 17–18, 20

fine arts, 12, 20

hospitality careers, 6–9, 15, 20

interests, 6, 8, 12, 17–21

literary arts, 12, 20

tourism careers, 6–9, 15, 20

ABOUT THE AUTHOR

Diane Lindsey Reeves writes books to help students of all ages find bright futures. She lives in North Carolina with her husband and a big kooky dog named Honey. She has four of the best grandkids in the world.